Treasure Island
Lit Link

Grades 7-8

Written by Nat Reed
Illustrated by Ric Ward

> **About the author:** Nat Reed has been a member of the teaching profession for over 30 years. He is presently a full-time instructor at Trent University in the Teacher Education Program.

ISBN 978-1-55035-894-0
Copyright 2007
All Rights Reserved * Printed in Canada

Published in the United States by:
On The Mark Press
3909 Witmer Road PMB 175
Niagara Falls, New York
14305
www.onthemarkpress.com

Published in Canada by:
S&S Learning Materials
15 Dairy Avenue
Napanee, Ontario
K7R 1M4
www.sslearning.com

At a Glance

Learning Expectations	Chapters 1-2	Chapters 3-4	Chapters 5-6	Chapters 7-8	Chapters 9-10	Chapters 11-12	Chapters 13-15	Chapters 16-17	Chapters 18-19	Chapters 20-21	Chapters 22-24	Chapters 25-27	Chapters 28-30	Chapters 31-32	Chapters 33-34
Reading Comprehension															
• Identify and describe story elements	•	•	•	•	•	•	•	•	•	•	•	•	•	•	•
• Summarize events/details	•	•	•	•	•	•	•	•	•	•	•	•	•	•	•
Reasoning & Critical Thinking Skills															
• Identify character traits and make comparisons	•	•		•	•		•	•							
• Identify setting	•														
• Use context clues (e.g., identify analogies)		•		•			•			•		•			
• Make inferences (e.g., why events occurred, characters' thoughts and feelings, etc.)		•		•	•	•		•	•		•	•	•	•	•
• Determine the meaning of colloquialisms and other phrases	•	•	•			•		•							
• Understand abstract concepts – conscience, revenge, fear, perseverance, self-respect, exaggeration, conflict, etc.		•		•				•	•	•		•	•		
• Develop opinions and personal interpretations	•	•		•	•			•				•			•
• Predict future events		•				•	•	•							•
• Write a letter/editorial for a newspaper								•				•			
• Conduct an interview										•					
• Develop research skills	•			•							•	•			
• Develop a poster/map/book cover												•		•	•
• Identify conflict/cliffhangers		•		•		•						•			
• Create a time line															•
• Identify quotations of characters													•		
Language Skills															
• Identify synonyms, antonyms, and homonyms		•								•	•	•			
• Identify similes		•											•		
• Identify personification/foreshadowing			•	•			•			•					
• Identify syllables/compound words		•													•
• Identify descriptive words and phrases		•		•	•							•	•	•	•
• Identify parts of speech										•	•				
• Use dictionary and thesaurus skills	•		•	•											•
• Use words correctly in sentences	•					•	•		•	•					
• Place words in alphabetical order				•											
• Identify plurals/root words				•						•					
• Use capitals and punctuation correctly					•										

Treasure Island

Robert Louis Stevenson

Table of Contents

Treasure Island
Robert Louis Stevenson

Overall Expectations

The students will:

- develop their skills in reading, writing, listening, and oral communication

- use good literature as a vehicle for developing skills required by curriculum expectations: reasoning and critical thinking, knowledge of language structure, vocabulary building, and use of conventions

- become meaningfully engaged in the drama of literature through a variety of types of questions and activities

- identify and describe elements of stories (e.g., plot, main idea, characters, setting)

- learn and review many skills in order to develop good reading habits

- provide clear answers to questions and well-constructed explanations

- organize and classify information to clarify thinking

- learn about the danger of making first impressions and the value of personal enterprise and bravery

- relate events and feelings found in novels to their own lives and experiences

- appreciate the importance of friendship and loyalty in personal relationships

- appreciate that the growth of one's character is more important than wealth or social status

- learn the importance of dealing with adversity and developing perseverance in the face of adversity

- state their own interpretation of a written work, using evidence from the work and from their own knowledge and experience

Treasure Island
Robert Louis Stevenson

List of Skills

Vocabulary Development

1. Identify/create similes
2. Locate descriptive words/phrases
3. List synonyms and antonyms
4. Use capitals and punctuation correctly
5. Identify syllables
6. List compound words
7. Use singular/plural nouns
8. Use context clues (analogies)
9. Identify parts of speech
10. Determine alphabetical order
11. Identify examples of personification
12. Identify root words

Setting Activities

1. Summarize the details of a setting
2. Create a treasure map
3. Create a time chart

Plot Activities

1. Complete a time line of events
2. Identify foreshadowing
3. Identify conflict in a story
4. Identify cliffhangers

Character Activities

1. Determine character traits
2. Compare two characters
3. Understand concepts such as perseverance, self-respect, courage, loyalty
4. Relate personal experiences

Creative and Critical Thinking

1. Research different topics
2. Write an editorial on an issue
3. Write a letter to a friend
4. Conduct an interview
5. Identify literary devices
6. Write a description of personal feelings
7. Design a poster
8. Design a treasure map
9. Design a cover for the novel
10. Determine the role of others in one's personal growth

Treasure Island

Robert Louis Stevenson

Teacher Suggestions

This resource can be used in a variety of ways:

1. The student booklet focuses on two to three chapters of the novel at a time. Each of these sections contains the following activities:

   a) Before you read the chapters (reasoning and critical thinking skills)
   b) Vocabulary building (dictionary and thesaurus skills)
   c) Questions on the chapter (reading comprehension skills)
   d) Language activities (grammar, punctuation, word structure, and extension activities)

2. Students may read the novel at their own speed and then select, or be assigned, a variety of questions and activities.

3. **Bulletin Board and Interest Center Ideas:** themes might include pirates, sailing ships and weaponry of the 18th Century, treasures, and deserted islands.

4. **Pre-Reading Activities:** *Treasure Island* may also be used in conjunction with themes of perseverance, honesty, loyalty in the face of adversity, and the danger of first impressions.

5. **Independent Reading Approach:** Students who are able to work independently may attempt to complete the assignments in a self-directed manner. Initially these students should participate in the pre-reading activities with the rest of the class. Students should familiarize themselves with the reproducible student booklet. Completed worksheets should be submitted so that the teacher can note how quickly and accurately the students are working. Students may be brought together periodically to discuss issues in specific sections of the novel.

6. **Fine Art Activities:** students may integrate such topics as desert islands, maps, pirates (flags, costumes), sailing ships, transportation, and weaponry of the 18th Century.

7. Encourage the students to keep a reading log in which they record their readings each day and their thoughts about the passage.

8. Students should keep all their work together in one place. A portfolio cover is provided for this reason.

9. Students should not be expected to complete all activities. Teachers should allow choice and in some cases match the activity to the student's ability.

10. Students should keep track (in their portfolio) of the activities they complete.

Treasure Island
Robert Louis Stevenson

Synopsis

Robert Louis Stevenson's *Treasure Island* is one of the most beloved novels ever written. Originally written in serial form in the late 1800s, it was an instant hit and since then has been read by countless people in many languages.

The principal figure of the novel is young Jim Hawkins. He and his recently-widowed mother run the Admiral Benbow Inn on the coast of England. When an old seaman, Billy Bones, dies at the inn, Jim discovers the treasure map of the famed Captain Flint among the old seaman's belongings. Knowing that the seaman's pirate friends know of the map, Jim quickly enlists the help of family friends Dr. Livesey and the squire. A sailing ship is purchased, a crew hired, and led by Captain Smollett, Jim and his friends head for the island on which the treasure is buried.

Upon reaching Treasure Island, Long John Silver, the ship's one-legged cook, leads most of the crew in a bloody mutiny against Captain Smollett and the others. After a number of scrimmages, the tide is finally turned against Long John and the mutineers. Victory is partially due to the help of Ben Gunn, a mysterious man who had been marooned on the island years earlier. With the treasure safely in the hold of the ship, Jim sets sail for home with his victorious friends. Long John is the only one of the mutineers to return from Treasure Island with Jim and the others, but escapes before the ship docks in England.

Author Biography

Robert Louis Stevenson

Robert Louis Stevenson is one of the most famous novelists ever to hail from Great Britain. Born in Edinburgh, Scotland, in 1850 he was constantly ill as a child, and was never very healthy throughout his life. From an early age Robert loved to read and wanted to spend his life as a writer. Because of his father's wishes, Robert studied to become a lawyer, but never really practiced law. Instead he wrote whenever he had the opportunity – poems, essays, and stories. Everyone who knew Robert considered him to be one of the nicest people they ever met. It was at the encouragement of his stepson, Lloyd Osbourn, that Robert wrote his first novel – the famed *Treasure Island*. In fact it was a real map of a Treasure Island that interested Robert in beginning his story of Long John Silver, Captain Flint, and Jim Hawkins. As Robert wrote the story he read each chapter aloud to his family, who even made suggestions. When first published it appeared chapter by chapter in the magazine called *Young Folks*. Stevenson originally called the novel *The Sea Cook*, and it was Stevenson's editor who suggested that the novel be titled *Treasure Island*. It achieved lasting popularity when published as a complete book.

Robert Louis Stevenson went on to write a number of immortal classics including *Kidnapped* and *The Strange Case of Dr. Jekyll and Mr. Hyde*, yet most unfortunately died when he was in his mid-40s. Nevertheless, his classic tales still live on today – most especially the wonderful and timeless novel, *Treasure Island*.

Treasure Island

Robert Louis Stevenson

Student Checklist

Student Name: _____

Assignment	Grade/Level	Comments

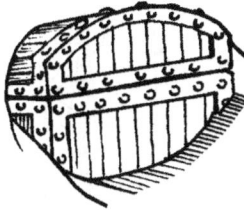

Treasure Island

Robert Louis Stevenson

Name: _____

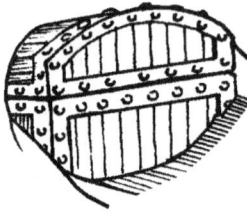

Treasure Island
Robert Louis Stevenson

Chapters 1 – 2

Before you read the chapters:

At one time the "scourge of the high seas" were the many pirates who sailed these waters. Find out at least three important facts about these people (e.g., what countries were they from, on whom did they prey, etc.).

_____

_____

_____

_____

Have you ever had the unpleasant experience of hosting an unwanted guest? Tell about such an experience, and how it might be resolved. Why can such a circumstance be extremely awkward?

_____

_____

_____

_____

Vocabulary:

1. Choose a word from the list to complete each sentence.

suffice	ruffian	effectual	precisely	incivility
tyrannize	abominable	connoisseur	indignant	rebuff

a) I'm sure that discriminating woman considers herself something of a _____ of the finer things in life.

b) The _____ weather stopped us from enjoying our vacation.

c) The cruel camp counselor made it his job to _____ all of the young campers in his care.

d) I'm sure that my aunt will _____ that man's advances.

e) The _____ stole her purse.

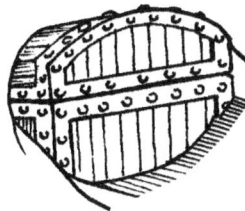

Treasure Island
Robert Louis Stevenson

f) The policeman's methods were most _____ in a crisis.

g) "There's no need for all of this _____," he said. "Why can't we all just get long?"

h) Even one million dollars will not _____ for that greedy person.

i) Poor Aunt Tessie was quite _____ at the imagined insult.

j) The bell will ring at _____ three o'clock.

2. A number of the words and phrases we meet in this novel are long out of use. Find out the meaning of the following examples:

a) "What mought you call me?" _____

b) "how that personage haunted my dreams" _____

c) "the Spanish Main" _____

d) "buy some stockings from a hawker" _____

e) "coltish country folk"_____

f) "the world will soon be quit of a very dirty scoundrel"_____

g) "would certainly have split him to the chine" _____

Questions:

1. Describe the setting of the first two chapters. Remember setting involves both place and time.

_____

_____

2. From the description given of the Captain when he first appears at the inn, list in point form four of these descriptors.

_____

_____

3. How did the captain terrorize everyone at the Admiral Benbow?

_____

_____

4. Why did the captain ask Jim to keep a watchful eye for a "seafaring man with one leg"?

_____

_____

5. Who was Black Dog?

_____

_____

6. Describe the captain's reaction to his meeting with Black Dog.

_____

_____

7. What dual role did Dr. Livesey have in the community?

_____

_____

Language Activities:

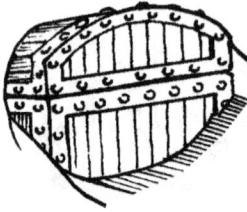

1. *Treasure Island* is perhaps the most famous novel about pirates ever written. Since Robert Louis Stevenson penned his great classic, however, a number of books and movies about pirates have come into existence. Think of another example of a book or movie on pirates and write a short synopsis of the plot.

_____

_____

_____

_____

_____

_____

_____

_____

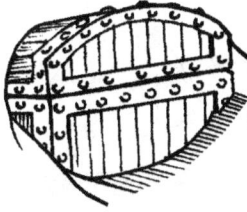

Treasure Island
Robert Louis Stevenson

2. A number of genuine pirates are still famous to this day. Choose one of the following buccaneers and research this person. Record information about their description and deeds in the following chart. Include at least five facts.

- Edward Teach (Blackbeard)
- Jean Laffite
- Anne Bonny
- Mary Read
- William Kidd
- Henry Morgan
- Francis Drake

Pirate:

_____

Sketch

Description:

_____

_____

_____

_____

_____

_____

_____

Deeds:

_____

_____

_____

_____

_____

_____

_____

Fate:

_____

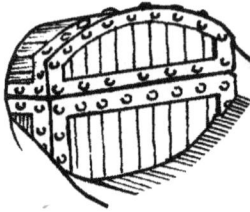

Treasure Island
Robert Louis Stevenson

Chapters 3 – 4

Before you read the chapters:

"The oldest and strongest emotion of mankind is fear." — *H.P. Lovecraft*
Describe a time in your own life when you experienced fear. In this incident, was fear a helpful emotion, or a destructive one? How so?

_____

_____

_____

_____

Vocabulary:

Using the words from the Word Box, complete the following crossword puzzle.

swab	Flint	bribe	Captain	repent	Livesey	Treasure
nimble	lugger	presume	detestable	pursue	tinder	gully
dell	doubloon	Stevenson	eight	fog	rat	pirates
Mate	greedy	bad	oars	sob		

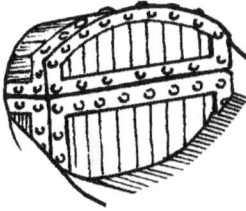

Treasure Island

Robert Louis Stevenson

Down

1. Something given to a person to obtain a favor
2. A small fishing boat
3. Despicable, hateful
4. An adjective that would describe Bill
5. Used to propel a rowboat
6. Agile
9. Famous pirate, Captain ___
13. To assume
15. Jim's family's physician
17. Buccaneers
19. To chase
21. A large knife

Across

3. A gold, Spanish coin
7. ____ Island
8. ___ box: materials for starting a fire
9. A foe of sailors everywhere
10. To cry
11. A small, wooded valley
12. To mop
14. This mammal overran many a pirate ship
16. To express you are sorry for something
18. A naval rank
20. Pieces of _____
22. To want more than you need
23. The First ____; next in rank to the Captain
24. Author of this novel

Questions:

1. What is revealed of Jim's character from the incident when the Captain offers Jim a bribe for getting him a drink of rum?

   _____

   _____

2. What was involved in being "tipped with the black spot"? Why did this frighten the Captain?

   _____

   _____

   _____

3. Why did Jim take the blind man to the Captain?

   _____

   _____

4. What was there about the blind beggar that was so frightening to Jim and his mother?

   _____

   _____

5. Describe the reception that Jim and his mother received at the hamlet.

   _____

   _____

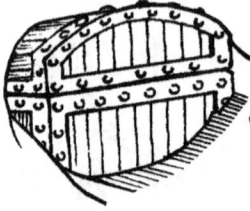

Treasure Island
Robert Louis Stevenson

6. Drawing on your own experiences, what are your thoughts on Jim's comment, "They say cowardice is infectious; but then argument is, on the other hand, a great emboldener"?

_____

_____

_____

7. When Jim and his mother arrived back at the inn after visiting the hamlet, what caused them to be in such a rush?

_____

_____

8. What do we learn about Jim's mother's character when they are going through the captain's trunk?

_____

_____

9. The conclusion of Chapter 4 is called a **cliffhanger**. Explain why.

_____

_____

_____

Language Activities:

An example of a **simile** (a comparison using like or as) is found in Chapter 3: "moving his legs like so much dead weight". In this example what two things are being compared?

_____

Come up with three similes of your own that have a definite *Treasure Island* flavor.

_____

_____

_____

_____

_____

_____

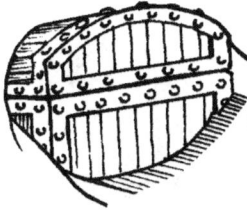

Treasure Island

Robert Louis Stevenson

Chapters 5 – 6

Before you read the chapters:

Look at the titles of the next two chapters. Predict what you think will happen in these chapters from these titles.

_____

_____

_____

_____

Vocabulary:

1. In each of the following sets of words, underline the one word that does not belong. Then write a sentence explaining why it does not fit.

   a) formidable   obsession   arduous   strenuous

   _____

   b) shirk   dodge   slack   probable

   _____

   c) cowardly   deplore   despise   hate

   _____

   d) proportion   share   readily   ratio

   _____

   e) condescending   menacing   patronizing   high-hatted

   _____

   f) prodigious   deliberate   great   extraordinary

   _____

   g) ambiguous   unclear   chancy   marked

   _____

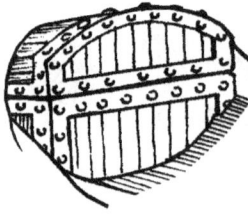

Treasure Island

Robert Louis Stevenson

2. Some of the words and expressions used in these chapters were peculiar to the time the novel was written. No longer do we hear these words in our everyday conversations. Using a dictionary, discover the meaning of the following (you may have to check the context):

a) skulk _____

b) squalling _____

c) glim _____

d) lubbers _____

e) dingle _____

f) son of a rum-puncheon _____

Questions:

Complete the following exercise filling in the correct words from the Word Box.

Trelawney	account	pigeon	tongue	Flint	revenue
map	horse	year	Dance	cabin	Pew
chest	Bill	Jim	Livesey	ship	

_____, the blind beggar, returned to the inn with a number of his companions. Inside the inn, they soon found out that _____ was dead. The blind man and the others were upset that they did not find "Flint's fist" in the dead man's _____. Enraged, the men decided to scour the area, searching for _____ and his mother. In the midst of their search, the owners of the inn were rescued by a group of _____officers. During the confusion, the blind man was killed by a _____. It turned out that Mr. _____ was the leader of the rescuers. Jim thought it best to take the paper he had saved from the chest to Dr. _____.

When Jim went to see Livesey, the magistrate was with Squire _____. A _____ pie was brought for Jim's supper. The men considered Captain _____

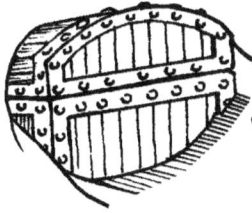

Treasure Island
Robert Louis Stevenson

to be the blood-thirstiest buccaneer that sailed. The squire swore that he would fit out a

_____ and search for the treasure if it took a _____. The book that

Jim had taken from the trunk was the pirate's _____ book. After examining the

_____, the men decided to go after the treasure. Jim would be the _____

boy. Livesey, however, was afraid that the squire would not be able to hold his _____.

Language Activities:

1. Reread the last two sentences of Chapter 6. How is this an example of foreshadowing?

   _____

   _____

2. Choose 10 words from these chapters with two or more **syllables**. Indicate the syllables by drawing a line between each syllable. **Example: some/where**

   _____   _____

   _____   _____

   _____   _____

   _____   _____

   _____   _____

3. Rummaging through an ancient chest belonging to a pirate must be a fascinating activity. Think of another interesting occupation (e.g., fighter pilot, astronaut, knight, king or queen, gunfighter of the old west, etc.). Now imagine going through this person's trunk like Jim did. What intriguing items might you find? Try to think of at least five possible artifacts.

   _____

   _____

   _____

   _____

   _____

   _____

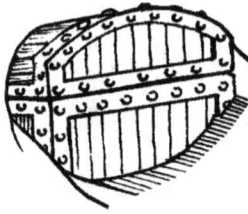

Treasure Island

Robert Louis Stevenson

Chapters 7 – 8

Before you read the chapters:

Trusting others with important responsibilities can sometimes lead to disappointing results. Describe an experience that you went through or heard about in which you entrusted someone else with a responsibility and ended up being "let down".

_____

_____

_____

Some of the people we meet in life are remembered most vividly for the remainder of our lives. Who do you think is the most interesting person you have ever met? What made this person so memorable?

_____

_____

_____

_____

Vocabulary:

Draw a straight line to connect the vocabulary word to its definition. Remember to use a straight edge (like a ruler).

1.	dexterity	a)	look forward to
2.	relinquish	b)	confuse
3.	confound	c)	clear
4.	anticipate	d)	petty officer
5.	transparent	e)	skill in physical movement
6.	indomitable	f)	relating to ships
7.	anecdote	g)	story
8.	nautical	h)	to give up something
9.	confidential	i)	unconquerable
10.	boatswain	j)	told in secret

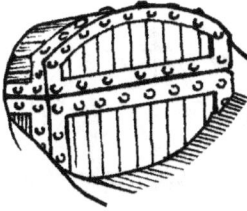

Treasure Island
Robert Louis Stevenson

Questions:

1. What did Jim spend much of his time dreaming about?

   _____

2. What was the name of the ship that the squire purchased?

   _____

3. What concern did Jim have when reading the squire's letter? Do you think this was a legitimate concern?

   _____

   _____

   _____

4. What sights did Jim enjoy in Bristol?

   _____

   _____

5. What was there about Long John Silver that set Jim's mind at ease?

   _____

   _____

6. What person from Jim's immediate past did he see in the Spy Glass Tavern?

   _____

7. When Long John was questioning Morgan about Black Dog, why do you suppose Morgan was asked leading questions throughout the interview?

   _____

   _____

8. What did Long John Silver find so funny about the incident with Black Dog?

   _____

   _____

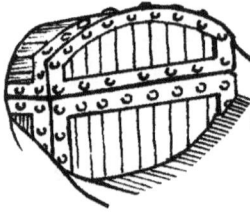

Treasure Island
Robert Louis Stevenson

Language Activities:

1. Find an example of foreshadowing from Jim's description of the island at the beginning of Chapter 7.

    _____

    _____

2. Write the plural of the following nouns from this chapter. Careful – you may wish to consult a dictionary for some of these words.

Singular Noun	Plural Noun
commentary	_____
wife	_____
opportunity	_____
punch	_____
man	_____
story	_____
rig	_____
gentleman	_____

3. Jim mentions in Chapter 7 that he despised Tom Redruth because the man could do nothing but grumble and lament. Certainly these are two very unappealing character traits. Think of another five traits of character that you find most disagreeable.

    _____

    _____

    _____

    _____

    _____

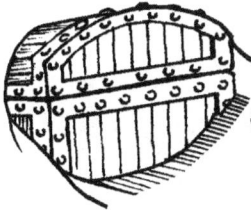

Treasure Island

Robert Louis Stevenson

Chapters 9 – 10

Before you read the chapters:

Have you ever had an experience when you had a "feeling" about a particular person or situation and everyone disagreed with you, yet you ended up being right? Describe what happened.

_____

_____

_____

_____

Vocabulary:

Choose a word from the list that means the same or nearly the same as the underlined word.

computation	duff	prosperous	intolerable	coxswain
capable	contrary	precaution	bowsprit	lanyard

1. The ship's captain found the stormy seas of the Atlantic most **unbearable**.   _____

2. He put his car into neutral as a **safeguard**.   _____

3. The **rich** industrialist was born in my hometown.   _____

4. The little boy seems quite **competent** at performing the simple task.   _____

5. A short **cord** was attached the key to his belt.   _____

6. The **helmsman** guided the ship through the narrow passage.   _____

7. Jim was knocked on the head with a wooden **spar**.   _____

8. **Pudding** was served to the crew on good days.   _____

9. By the first mate's **calculation**, they were nearing the Equator.   _____

10. **Counter** to popular opinion, the Earth turned out to be round.   _____

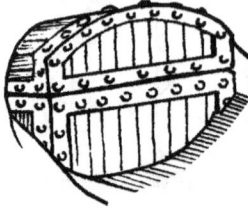

Treasure Island
Robert Louis Stevenson

Questions:

1. What three things concerned Captain Smollett?

   _____

   _____

2. Why do you think the squire took the captain's concerns so personally?

   _____

   _____

3. What do you think of the captain's complaint that he should have had a say in the choosing of the ship's crew?

   _____

   _____

4. The squire swore that he had told no one the longitude and latitude of the island. If he had not told anyone, how do you think the crew found out?

   _____

   _____

5. Describe the kind of first mate that Mr. Arrow turned out to be. What was his fate?

   _____

   _____

   _____

6. What was Long John Silver's nickname? How do you suppose he came by this name?

   _____

   _____

7. Long John claims that his parrot is 200 years old. Investigate to find out if Long John's claim could be true.

   _____

   _____

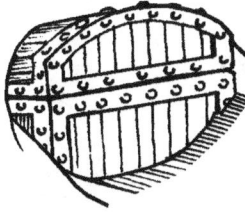

Treasure Island

Robert Louis Stevenson

8. Describe how Chapter 10 ends as a **cliffhanger**.

_____

_____

Language Activities:

1. Place the following words from these chapters in alphabetical order.

saluted   _____

sailor   _____

Smollett   _____

Silver   _____

shipshape   _____

stay   _____

ship   _____

sir   _____

mutiny   _____

soon   _____

2. Complete the following chart by selecting words from Chapter 9 and 10.

Find five different proper nouns (e.g., names of people of places)	
Find five verbs (e.g., action words)	
Find five adjectives (descriptive words)	
Find five words peculiar to pirates, sailors, or the time in which the novel was written	
Find five pronouns (words that replace nouns)	

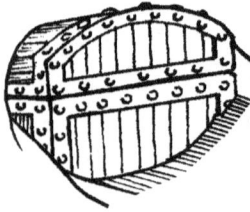

Treasure Island
Robert Louis Stevenson

Chapters 11 – 12

Before you read the chapters:

From the concluding statement of Chapter 10, it is obvious that what Jim overhears in the apple barrel is of critical importance to himself and his friends. Before reading this chapter, predict what you think Jim overheard in the apple barrel.

_____

_____

_____

_____

Vocabulary:

Solve the following word search puzzle using the words from the Word Box. Remember, the words can be horizontal, vertical, or diagonal. They may be forward or even backward!

Flint	England	corruption	quid	Smollett	foresail	careen
skeleton	Livesey	silver	parrot	barrel	captain	Hawkins

```
q u i d q w e r t y u i o p a
a f s d f e n g l a n d f s g
s z l x c v b n i n m q w n g
k w e i r t y u v u i o p i n
e q w e n f o r e s a i l k o
l a s d f t f g s g h n j w i
e x x c s i l v e r v i p a t
t b n m q w e r y t y a u h p
o s m o l l e t t a r t s d u
n d f g g h j k l r l p q w r
z x n e e r a c o x c a v b r
q x w e r t y t y u u c i o o
b a r r e l a s d f g h j p c
```

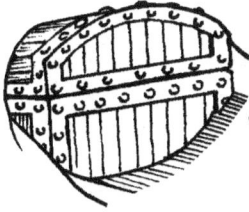

Treasure Island
Robert Louis Stevenson

Questions:

1. As briefly as possible summarize what Jim overheard when he was hiding in the apple barrel.

   _____

   _____

2. Why didn't Long John Silver put all of his savings in the same place?

   _____

   _____

3. What was Long John Silver implying about his own character by saying that Captain Flint was afraid of him?

   _____

4. When did the plotters plan to take over the ship?

   _____

   _____

5. Why did Long John Silver feel they needed Captain Smollett?

   _____

   _____

6. What did Long John Silver feel was the undoing of many such mutinous plans?

   _____

   _____

7. What became of Captain Flint?

   _____

8. How did Jim arrange to meet Dr. Livesey and the others to tell them about the plot?

   _____

   _____

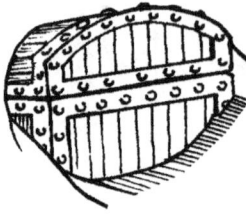

9. What was there about this mutiny that Captain Smollett considered so remarkable?

_____

_____

Language Activities:

1. Put the following unusual words or expressions into your own words (you may have to check the context):

   a) "there's my hand on it now" _____

   _____

   b) "Dick's square" _____

   _____

   c) "I never clapped my eyes on" _____

   _____

   d) "Jim is a noticing lad" _____

   _____

2. Rewrite the following sentences putting in the correct **capitalization** and **punctuation**.

   a) the crew of the hispaniola was overjoyed to reach skeleton island

   _____

   b) long john silver gave jim a ferocious glare

   _____

   c) why don't you go to victoria british columbia at christmas

   _____

   d) aunt eileen was born in turkey

   _____

   e) chester crossed the states of nevada and california before reaching the pacific ocean

   _____

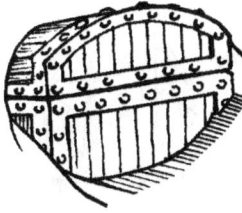

Treasure Island
Robert Louis Stevenson

Chapters 13 – 15

Before you read the chapters:

As the Hispaniola approaches *Treasure Island*, Jim and his friends find themselves in a very dangerous position. Predict what you think will happen to them in the next few chapters.

_____

_____

_____

_____

Vocabulary:

Write a sentence using the following words. Make sure that the meaning of the word is clear in your sentence.

melancholy – _____

_____

conceal – _____

_____

contort – _____

_____

simultaneous – _____

_____

extricate – _____

_____

adversary – _____

_____

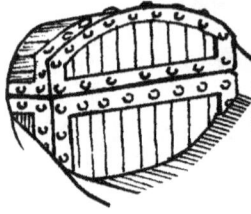

Treasure Island

Robert Louis Stevenson

cannibals –

proportion –

pious –

Questions:

Answer the following questions by indicating whether each statement is **True** or **False**.

1. When the Hispaniola arrived at Skeleton Island the crew were all in a happy frame of mind. T or F

2. Dr. Livesey thought it was a most unhealthy place. T or F

3. Three crewmen, Hunter, Joyce, and Redruth, were taken into the confidence of the squire. T or F

4. Captain Smollett allowed most of the crew to go ashore. T or F

5. Jim tried to sneak aboard one of the boats going ashore. T or F

6. On the island, Jim witnessed Long John Silver kill Smollett. T or F

7. When Jim first saw Ben Gunn, he thought him to be a cannibal. T or F

8. Ben Gunn ended up on the island because of a shipwreck. T or F

9. Ben told Jim that he had already discovered the treasure. T or F

10. Jim and Ben were discovered together by Long John Silver who took them captive. T or F

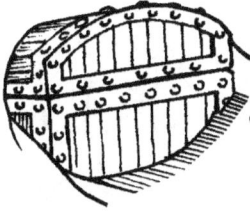

Treasure Island

Robert Louis Stevenson

Language Activities:

1. Chapter 13 features at least two examples of the literary device known as **personification** (writing about an inanimate object as if it was a person).

   Explain why each of the following descriptions are examples of this literary device:

   a) "the general coloring was uniform and sad"

   _____

   _____

   b) "perhaps it was the look of the island, with its gray, melancholy woods..."

   _____

   _____

2. We have already read about a number of important conflicts in this novel. **Conflict** is an important element in a novel. There are generally three types of conflict: **person against person**, **person against self**, and **person against nature**. Find three examples of conflict in *Treasure Island*, illustrating these three types.

   a) Person against Person: _____

   _____

   _____

   b) Person against Self:_____

   _____

   _____

   c) Person against Nature: _____

   _____

   _____

3. On a separate sheet of paper, draw a picture of Skeleton Island that shows the features and mood described in the chapter.

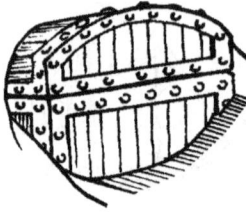

Treasure Island

Robert Louis Stevenson

Chapters 16 – 17

Before you read the chapters:

Look at the chapter titles for these two chapters. Using only this information, what do you think will happen in this section?

_____

_____

_____

_____

Vocabulary:

Choose a word from the list to complete each sentence. You may have to check the context of the words from these chapters.

invaluable	instincts	proceeded	palisade	knoll
consultation	besiege	gig	leeward	scuffle

1. To _____ a fortress is to surround it.

2. Before making important decisions, it is often wise to organize a _____.

3. If I'm facing the direction toward which the wind is blowing, I'm facing _____.

4. A _____ is the name for a rowboat.

5. It is not always a good idea to follow your _____.

6. A little hill is also called a _____.

7. "I'm sure what is found in the treasure chest will prove _____," the doctor said.

8. The boys _____ down the street on their bikes.

9. Jim found a large wooden _____ on the island.

10. The pirate was disarmed after a brief _____.

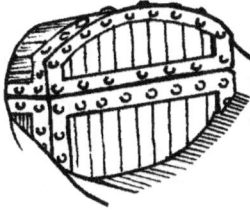

Treasure Island
Robert Louis Stevenson

Questions:

1. Who takes over as the narrator of the novel in Chapter 16? Why do you think the author makes this switch?

   _____

   _____

   _____

2. What advantage would the stockade be to whichever side took possession of it?

   _____

   _____

3. What was the one thing they lacked among the stores taken ashore from the ship?

   _____

   _____

4. Describe how Abraham Gray came to join the squire's men.

   _____

   _____

5. Describe what happened that presented a great deal of danger to Dr. Livesey and the others on their fifth trip ashore.

   _____

   _____

6. Who was the best shot among Livesey's men? Why did they need to call upon him at this time?

   _____

   _____

7. Describe the predicament Livesey and the others found themselves in at the conclusion of Chapter 17.

   _____

   _____

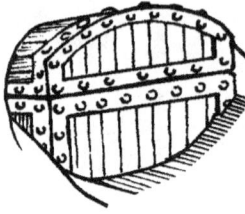

Treasure Island
Robert Louis Stevenson

Language Activities:

1. Jim's life certainly got a lot more exciting when the Captain came to stay at the inn. Using a separate sheet of paper, imagine that you are Jim and are **writing a letter** to your friend back in England. Describe all the exciting things that have happened to you and how you ended up on a pirate's ship on a mysterious island looking for buried treasure.

2. Using the comparison framework below, compare two of the characters that you have met thus far in *Treasure Island*. Please consider both the personalities and physical features of these two people.

Characteristics	Character #1	Character #2

3. Imagine that the author decided to continue using Jim's point of view for these chapters instead of the doctor's. Describe how Stevenson might have arranged the plot so that Jim was present to witness these events.

_____

_____

_____

_____

_____

_____

_____

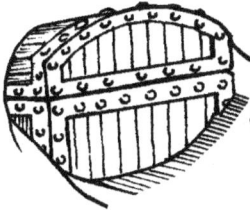

Treasure Island

Robert Louis Stevenson

Chapters 18 – 19

Before you read the chapters:

Who do you think would have the advantage in the novel to this point: Jim and his friends on the island, or Long John Silver and his pirates who control the ship? Explain your answer.

_____

_____

_____

_____

Vocabulary:

Synonyms are words with similar meanings. Using the context of the sentences below, choose the best synonym or meaning for the underlined words in each sentence.

1. The prisoner accepted his orders with **acquiescence**.
    a) passivity   b) anger   c) surprise   d) complaint

2. He held his girlfriend's picture most **reverently**.
    a) selfishly   b) cautiously   c) respectfully   d) determinedly

3. We wanted to show our enemies that we **despised** their attack.
    a) hated   b) loved   c) laughed-at   d) looked forward to

4. He found that he had an **ally** in Ben Gunn.
    a) enemy   b) friend   c) turncoat   d) dependant

5. I didn't think the wound was as **severe** as it turned out to be.
    a) deep   b) shallow   c) bloody   d) serious

6. He didn't **venture** to try the sport again.
    a) sacrifice himself   b) go outside   c) attempt   d) go aboard

7. They found the store had been **demolished** over the weekend.
    a) destroyed   b) purchased   c) sold   d) sacrificed

8. Arriving at the stockade, they found the **magazine** empty.
    a) small booklet   b) arsenal   c) office   d) port

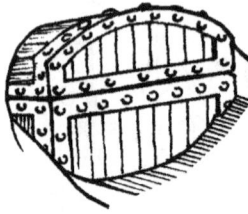

Treasure Island

Robert Louis Stevenson

Questions:

1. Describe what happened to Redruth.

   _____

   _____

2. What had been Redruth's occupation back in England?

   _____

   _____

3. Why did Captain Smollett "run up the colors" at the stockade?

   _____

   _____

4. Why did this turn out to be a dangerous thing to do?

   _____

   _____

5. When was the soonest that the squire expected help from his friends in England?

   _____

   _____

6. Why do you think the Captain kept writing in his log even when they weren't aboard the ship?

   _____

   _____

7. How did Ben Gunn know it was Jim's friends in the stockade?

   _____

   _____

8. Describe the proposal that Ben Gunn made to Jim.

   _____

   _____

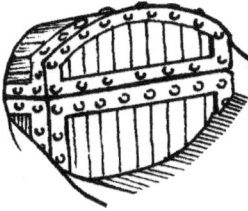

Treasure Island
Robert Louis Stevenson

9. What had Ben Gunn hidden by the white rock?

_____

10. What does it tell you about the squire when he says of Smollett, "He is a better man than I am. And when I say that, it means a great deal, Jim"?

_____

_____

Language Activities:

1. The author has a very imaginative way of expressing himself. Rewrite the following sentences from these chapters in your own words:

   a) "If I durst," said the captain.

   _____

   b) "The captain made us trim the boat."

   _____

   c) "And you're all in a clove hitch, ain't you?"

   _____

   d) "I'm back on piety."

   _____

2. Copy out any three sentences from these chapters and underline the verbs.

   _____

   _____

   _____

   _____

   _____

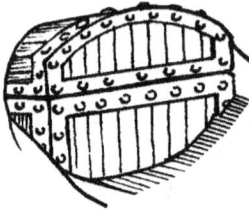

3. Beside each of the following words from this chapter, write its root word.

molestation _____ apologetically _____

serviceable _____ lying _____

wading _____ observation _____

peculiarity _____ livelier _____

4. An exciting action scene must be skillfully written by the author. Robert Louis Stevenson certainly is a master at describing such a scene.

   a) Think of two things you think are essential for an author to include when describing an action scene.

   _____

   _____

   b) Rewrite the following two sentences so that they are more exciting:

   Long John Silver drew his sword and tried to use it on the first mate.

   _____

   _____

   Jim Hawkins joined the battle by swinging down from the top sail on a rope.

   _____

   _____

   c) Write your own exciting action scene.

   _____

   _____

   _____

   _____

   _____

   _____

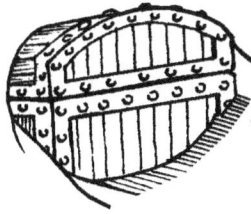

Treasure Island

Robert Louis Stevenson

Chapters 20 – 21

Before you read the chapters:

"One of the truest tests of integrity is its blunt refusal to be compromised." – *Chinua Achebe*

Do you think the quote by Chinua Achebe is always true? Defend your answer.

_____

_____

_____

_____

Vocabulary:

1. **Antonyms** are words with opposite meanings. Draw a line from each word in Column A to its antonym in Column B.

Column A	Column B
evident	stormy
immense	logical
promotion	tiny
placid	loyal
absurd	ceased
resumed	demotion
treacherous	hidden

2. Use the words in column A to fill in the blanks in the sentences below.

   a) Long John Silver proved to be a most _____ man.

   b) Due to his faithful service, he earned a _____ to admiral.

   c) The very notion that he was disloyal is quite _____.

   d) My uncle eats an _____ amount of food.

   e) It is quite _____ that she was not being sincere.

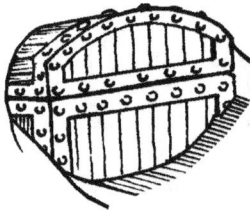
Treasure Island
Robert Louis Stevenson

f) The lake is usually quite _____ first thing in the morning.

g) The robin _____ her search for worms as soon as the rain let up.

Questions:

Indicate whether the following statements are **True** or **False**.

1. Silver's pet parrot was injured during his peace talks in the stockade. **T** or **F**

2. In Chapter 20 Ben Gunn climbed aboard the ship and blew it up. **T** or **F**

3. Silver accused Captain Smollett of desertion. **T** or **F**

4. Silver was quite rude to Jim when they met during the negotiations. **T** or **F**

5. In exchange for the map, Silver would let them have the ship. **T** or **F**

6. No one helped Silver to his feet after the negotiations. **T** or **F**

7. Captain Smollett took charge of their defense before the battle. **T** or **F**

8. Joyce, Hunter, and the Captain were all wounded in the fight. **T** or **F**

9. The pirates were driven off. **T** or **F**

10. Although they won the battle, the stockade was burned to the ground. **T** or **F**

Language Activities:

1. Find five examples of the following parts of speech from these chapters.

Nouns	Verbs	Adjectives
_____	_____	_____
_____	_____	_____
_____	_____	_____
_____	_____	_____
_____	_____	_____

Treasure Island
Robert Louis Stevenson

2. Interview at least three other students for their views of this novel. (Try to get both positive and negative comments.) Write a brief report putting these views together.

Interview 1: _____
_____
_____
_____

Interview 2: _____
_____
_____
_____

Interview 3: _____
_____
_____
_____

Report: _____
_____
_____
_____
_____
_____
_____
_____
_____
_____
_____
_____

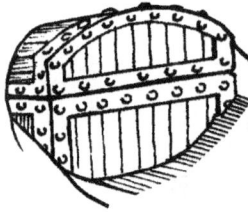

Treasure Island

Robert Louis Stevenson

Chapters 22 – 24

Before you read the chapters:

During the days of Long John Silver, Captain Flint, and other famous buccaneers, there was a multitude of ships and boats sailing the world's ocean waters. In this chapter Jim makes use of a homemade boat called a coracle. Research the coracle or another type of boat (large or small) and come up with three important features of that particular craft.

_____

_____

_____

_____

_____

_____

Vocabulary:

Analogies are equations in which the first pair of words has the same relationship as the second pair of words. For example, **stop** is to **go** as **fast** is to **slow**. In this example, both pairs of words are opposites. Choose the best word from the word box to complete each of the analogies below.

obstinate	reverberations	hawser	repulse	admirable
supervene	variable	yaw	grievous	precaution

1. **Serious** is to _____ as **old** is to **aged**.

2. **Safety measure** is to _____ as **car** is to **automobile**.

3. **Disgraceful** is to _____ as **wild** is to **tame**.

4. **Constant** is to _____ as **rare** is to **usual**.

5. **Smile** is to **grin** as **stubborn** is to _____.

6. **Attract** is to _____ as **forget** is to **remember**.

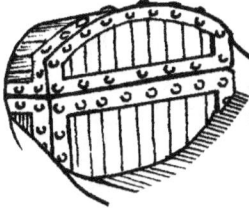

Treasure Island
Robert Louis Stevenson

7. **Despondent** is to **sad** as **rope** is to _____.

8. **Vibrations** are to _____ as **silly** is to **inane**.

9. **Stop** is to **cease** as **result** is to _____.

10. **Swerve** is to _____ as **beautiful** is to **lovely**.

Questions:

1. At the beginning of Chapter 22, what did Dr. Livesey do that surprised Jim and the others?

_____

_____

2. Describe Ben Gunn's boat.

_____

_____

3. What did Jim find unpleasant about being stuck in the stockade?

_____

_____

4. Describe Jim's daring plan regarding the Hispaniola.

_____

_____

5. What prevented him from cutting the "hawser"?

_____

_____

6. Do you think Jim's plan regarding the Hispaniola was very smart? Why?

_____

_____

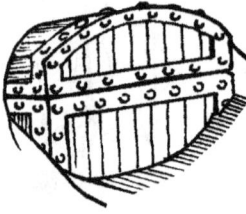

7. Describe what was going on inside the ship when Jim got there.

_____

_____

8. What was it that made Jim afraid to land his little boat on the island?

_____

_____

Language Activities:

1. There is an interesting example of **personification** (writing about inanimate objects as if they were a person) in Chapter 23:

" … was a very safe boat for a person of my height and weight, both buoyant and clever in a seaway".

  a) Why is this an example of personification?

  _____

  _____

  b) Put on your pirate's hat and black eye patch and come up with two more piratey examples of this literary device of your own (e.g., the Jolly Roger flapping in the breeze, a pirate's cutlass during a sword fight, the sounds a pirate's ship makes during a storm).

  _____

  _____

  _____

  _____

2. Another sea chantey is mentioned in this section:

"But one man of her crew alive,
What put to sea with seventy-five."

Using your imagination, create a similar **couplet** as this example describing Jim Hawkins' adventures thus far.

_____

_____

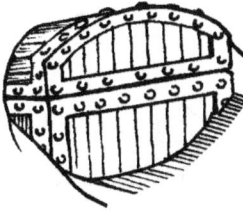

Treasure Island
Robert Louis Stevenson

Chapters 25 – 27

Before you read the chapters:

In these chapters Jim disobeys the orders of Captain Smollett and suffers the consequences. Why is it usually important to obey the rules of those in authority?

_____

_____

Is it ever a good idea to disobey such rules? Explain.

_____

_____

_____

Vocabulary:

Circle the **most** correct meaning (**synonym**) for each underlined word.

1. The science teacher found the student's remark most **derisive**.
   a) sarcastic   b) pleasant   c) scornful   d) comical

2. Israel Hand's actions were **treacherous**.
   a) dangerous   b) loving   c) wise   d) intricate

3. Jim was wise to the **deception** that Israel tried on him.
   a) suffering   b) joke   c) wonderment   d) trick

4. As a **precaution**, the ladder was placed by the window.
   a) celebration   b) safeguard   c) testament   d) decoration

5. I saw no hope of any **ultimate** escape.
   a) quick   b) soon   c) final   d) surprise

6. He was still wearing the same look of extreme **perplexity**.
   a) confusion   b) amusement   c) dismay   d) anger

7. I **desisted** with a violent shudder.
   a) started   b) stopped   c) paused   d) cried out

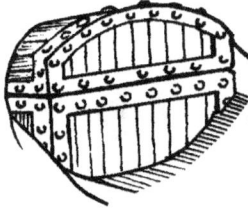

Treasure Island
Robert Louis Stevenson

8. I walked more **circumspectly**, keeping an eye on every side.

   a) quietly   **b)** bravely   **c)** noisily   **d)** cautiously

9. We found a **convenient** place to stop for the night.

   a) handy   **b)** cheap   **c)** quiet   **d)** recommended

10. Captain Smollett wanted some **assurance** from the pirates that they could be trusted.

   a) treasure   **b)** keepsake   **c)** guarantee   **d)** license

Questions:

1. What does the title of Chapter 25 mean?

_____

_____

2. Describe what Jim saw when he climbed aboard the Hispaniola.

_____

_____

3. How did Israel Hands try to deceive Jim?

_____

_____

4. What sort of partnership did Jim and Israel briefly form? Why?

_____

_____

5. Why did Jim's pistol misfire when he first tried to use it?

_____

6. Describe the fate of Israel Hands.

_____

_____

7. What shock awaited Jim when he climbed into the stockade late that night?

_____

_____

8. Chapter 27 ends as a real cliffhanger. Describe what you think will happen next in the story.

_____

_____

_____

_____

Language Activities:

1. Investigate to find out the duties of the coxswain.

_____

_____

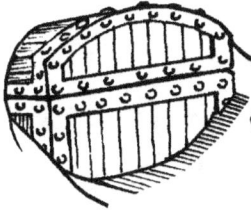

2. Imagine that you are a newspaper editor for *The London Times* back in the 1700s and you are writing an editorial on the topic of Jim Hawkin's voyage to Treasure Island. Like many of your readers who have learned of Jim's trip aboard the Hispaniola, you are quite interested in the fact that the squire and Dr. Livesey would take a young boy on such a dangerous voyage.

   Write an editorial expressing your point of view in this matter. Use the space below to develop your arguments, then write your editorial out in full on a separate sheet of paper. You may choose to defend Jim's participation in the adventure (despite the dangers) or express concerns that Jim's mother and these two distinguished gentlemen would risk Jim's life on such a venture. Remember your job is to convince your readers regarding your point of view in this matter.

   State your point of view: _____

   _____

   Your supporting arguments: _____

   _____

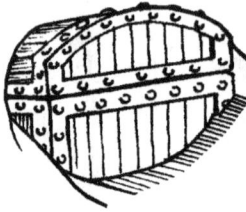

Your supporting arguments (cont'd) _____

_____

_____

_____

_____

_____

2. Design a **wanted poster** advertising a reward for the capture of one of the famous pirates of the 1700s. Your poster should include a sketch of the buccaneer of your choice, pertinent information about him or her, the amount of the reward, and who should be contacted if this person is killed, captured, or even spotted.

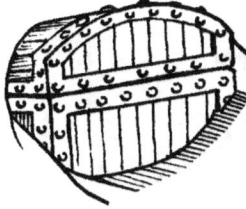

Treasure Island

Robert Louis Stevenson

3. *Treasure Island* is a fascinating novel filled with exotic places, people, and events. **With one or two classmates** discuss some of the most interesting things you have encountered thus far in your reading of the novel. With your group, brainstorm two or three things that you would like to learn more about (e.g., pirate ships, buried treasure, famous pirates). Narrow your selection down to one interesting topic that your group would like to know more about. Before beginning your research, your group should complete the first two columns of the KWL Chart below – then your group should complete the last column after doing your research.

Topic:

What I Know	What I Want to Know	What I Learned

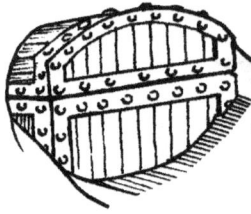

Treasure Island
Robert Louis Stevenson

Chapters 28 – 30

Before you read the chapters:

Jim finds himself confronted by his enemies in these chapters and is forced to quickly decide how to approach this desperate situation. Should he try to talk or explain his way out of his circumstances, or should he just tell the pirates the truth and hope for the best? Defend your choice.

_____

_____

_____

_____

Vocabulary:

In each of the following sets of words, underline the one word that does not belong. Then write a sentence explaining why it does not fit.

1. apprehension	freedom	alarm	dread
2. consumed	composure	coolness	nonchalance
3. truculent	hostile	belligerent	talented
4. furtive	sneaky	weak	sly
5. sincere	incongruous	inconsistent	incompatible
6. contempt	enjoyment	disdain	scorn

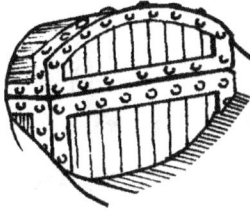
Treasure Island
Robert Louis Stevenson

7. vehemence   fury   circumstance   intensity

_____

8. perilous   dangerous   hazardous   stupendous

_____

Questions:

1. At the beginning of Chapter 28, what did Jim think happened to Dr. Livesey and his other friends?

_____

_____

2. Why were his friends upset with him at this point in the story?

_____

_____

3. Why do you think Jim told Long John Silver the whole story of how he found out about the pirates' plans?

_____

_____

4. Explain why Long John Silver defended Jim when the other pirates wanted to kill him?

_____

_____

5. What did the "black spot" mean?

_____

_____

6. What does the title of Chapter 30, "On Parole", mean in the story?

_____

_____

7. Why do you think that the doctor came to the stockade to tend to the sick and injured?

_____

_____

8. What did Dr. Livesey suggest that Jim do right away when they were speaking by themselves?

_____

Language Activities:

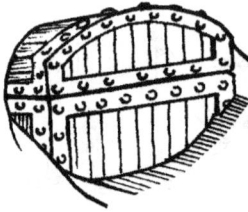

1. With a straight line, match each character from *Treasure Island* with a quotation made by that character. (These quotations go back to the beginning of the novel.)

a) Silver

b) Jim

c) Captain Flint

d) Dr. Livesey

e) Smollett

f) Israel Hands

g) Ben Gunn

1. "As you have brewed so shall you drink, my boy."

2. "I'll engage to clap you all in irons, and take you home to a fair trial."

3. "I've seen too many die since I fell in with you."

4. "I haven't spoke with a Christian these three years."

5. "Here's Jim Hawkins, shiver my timbers"

6. "Dead men don't bite; them's my views."

7. "Pieces of eight. Pieces of eight."

2. There are a number of examples of **similes** (a comparison using the words like or as) in this novel, for example:

"looking fit and taut as a fiddle"

Create your own similes to describe the following:

a) a graceful dive:_____

b) the speed of a gazelle: _____

c) the cruelty of Long John Silver: _____

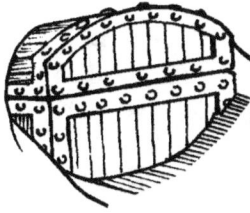

Treasure Island

Robert Louis Stevenson

Chapters 31 – 32

Before you read the chapters:

Tell about a time when you or a friend were really scared. Be sure to include the circumstances.

_____

_____

_____

_____

How did you react (mind and body) to the situation?

_____

_____

_____

Vocabulary:

Draw a straight line to connect the vocabulary word to its definition. Remember to use a straight edge (like a ruler).

1.	precaution	a)	fear
2.	feasible	b)	cliff
3.	subsist	c)	exist
4.	apprehension	d)	luxury
5.	inexplicable	e)	tied
6.	ambiguity	f)	wariness
7.	tethered	g)	aloud
8.	precipice	h)	uncertainty
9.	volubly	i)	possible
10.	extravagance	j)	difficult to account for

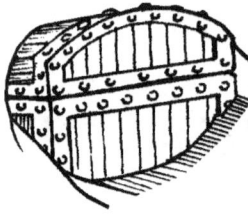

Treasure Island

Robert Louis Stevenson

Questions:

1. What had Long John Silver observed when watching Jim and the doctor conversing that had impressed him?

   _____

   _____

2. After their meeting with Dr. Livesey in Chapter 31, Long John Silver was in a fine humor. Why was Jim still worried?

   _____

   _____

3. After breakfast, what did Long John Silver and the pirates set out to do?

   _____

   _____

4. Under what object did they think the treasure had been buried?

   _____

   _____

5. **a)** What startling discovery did they make at the bottom of a large pine tree?

   _____

   b) What did Long John suppose it meant?

   _____

   _____

6. What else frightened the pirates when they approached the spot where the treasure was buried?

   _____

   _____

7. What do you think happened to the treasure?

   _____

   _____

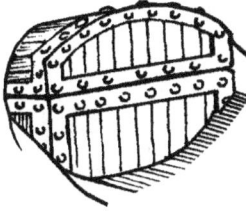

Treasure Island

Robert Louis Stevenson

Language Activities:

1. Try to reassemble the word parts listed below into ten compound words which are found in this chapter.

mess	out	least	with	any	mizzen	tree	tops	it	back
man	ways	mates	day	thing	light	mast	self	gentle	ward

a) _____ f) _____

b) _____ g) _____

c) _____ h) _____

d) _____ i) _____

e) _____ j) _____

2. Create a **map** indicating a buried treasure in an area with which you are very familiar. Be sure to include a compass rose, distinguishing landmarks to assist potential treasure-seekers, and written and/or visual instructions to the mother lode.

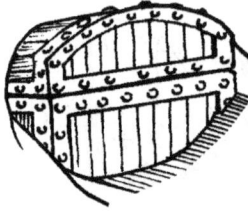

Treasure Island

Robert Louis Stevenson

Chapters 33 – 34

Before you read the chapters:

What do you think would be a suitable fate for Long John Silver?

_____

_____

What do you think will happen to him?

_____

_____

_____

_____

Vocabulary:

Use a dictionary to find the meanings of the following words:

insolence – _____

excavation – _____

leisurely – _____

profound – _____

prodigious – _____

dereliction – _____

obsequious – _____

ingratiate – _____

demolish – _____

escapade – _____

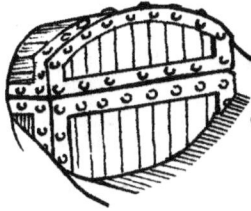

Treasure Island
Robert Louis Stevenson

Questions:

Complete the following paragraph with the correct words from these two chapters.

eight	shots	four	three	retired	Flint	ship	
cave	pig-nuts	Ben Gunn	pistol	Merry	Captain Smollett		
Long John Silver	one thousand	Hispaniola					

Before the buccaneers began digging in the pit for the treasure, Long John Silver passed
Jim a _____. Long John suggested that the buccaneers would only find
some _____ in the hole. George _____ was the leading
spokesman for the pirates. The pirates were about to charge Long John and Jim when
three _____ from the thicket suddenly interrupted them. Silver was very
surprised to see his old shipmate, _____, with Dr. Livesey. It had turned
out that Ben Gunn had carried the treasure from its burial spot to his _____.
Just inside the mouth of the North Inlet they met the _____, cruising by
herself. When Jim and the others finally left the island, they left the _____
mutineers behind. Even though he was still recovering from his wounds, _____
was still the leader on the voyage home. At a port in Spanish America, _____
managed to escape. Only _____ men who had started the voyage to Treasure Island
finally returned to England. Ben Gunn received _____ pounds, which he spent
or lost in _____ weeks. After the voyage, Captain Smollett _____
from the sea, and Gray purchased a _____. As for Jim, for years after the
voyage he heard the voice of Captain _____ in his dreams, "Pieces of
_____, pieces of _____."

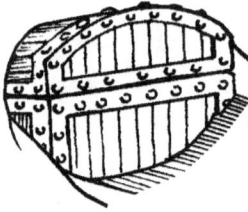

Treasure Island

Robert Louis Stevenson

Language Activities:

1. Pirates are essentially thieves and murderers. And yet they have been romanticized in many novels and movies.

   a) What does it mean to romanticize something?

   _____

   _____

   b) Why do you think pirates have been romanticized?

   _____

   _____

   _____

   _____

2. On a separate sheet, create a **book cover** for *Treasure Island*. Be sure to include the title, author, and a picture that will make other students want to read the novel.

3. List the main events of *Treasure Island* in time order.

Treasure Island – Main Events
First _____
Next _____
Next _____
Next _____
Next _____
Next _____
Next _____
Next _____
Next _____
Last _____

Answer Key

Chapters 1 – 2: *(page 10)*

Vocabulary:

1. a) connoisseur   b) abominable   c) tyrannize   d) rebuff   e) ruffian
   f) effectual   g) incivility   h) suffice   i) indignant   j) precisely
2. a) might   b) person
   c) the mainland coast of the Spanish Empire around the Caribbean
   d) peddler   e) full of fun   f) soon be rid   g) chin

Questions:

1. 18th Century on the coast of England at the Admiral Benbow Inn.
2. tall, strong, heavy, nut-brown, tarry pigtail falling over his shoulder, hands ragged and scarred, broken, black nails, saber cut across one cheek
3. He was often drunk, loud, bossy and threatening.
4. Answers may vary (e.g., the Captain was hiding from him).
5. A sailor who visited the inn looking for the Captain.
6. He looked like he'd seen a ghost.
7. He was a physician and magistrate.

Language Activities:

1. Answers may vary. For example, book – *Peter Pan*, movie – *Pirates of the Caribbean*, play –*The Pirates of Penzance.*

Chapters 3 – 4: *(page 14)*

Vocabulary:

```
 1b          2l      3d o u 4b l 5o o 6n
 7T r e a s u r e        a     a     i
  i          g    8t i n d e r       m
  b      9F o g e           10S o b
11d e l l       12s w a b           l
13p      i    14r a t   15L          e
16r e 17p e n t      18C a p t a i n
  e   i    19p b l           v
  s   r    u  l    20e i 21g h t
  u   a  22g r e e d y  s  u
23M a t e     s      e  l
  e   e       u      y  l
     24S t e v e n s o n    y
```

Questions:

1. He is honorable and honest.
2. It was a summons.
3. He forced Jim by wrenching his arm.
4. Answers may vary (e.g., he was evil and seemed capable of anything).
5. No one was interested in helping them.
6. Answers may vary.
7. They had only until ten o'clock, when the blind man and his friends would return.
8. She would only take what was owed her (e.g., honest).
9. The chapter ends at the point where Jim and his mother are in extreme danger from the blind man and the others, and we are anxious to find out what will happen to them.

Chapters 5 – 6: *(page 17)*

Vocabulary:

1. a) obsession – the other words all mean **difficult to undertake**
   b) probable – the other words all mean **to avoid or neglect**

c) cowardly – the other words all mean **to feel or express a strong disapproval of**
d) readily – the other words all mean **a part of something**
e) menacing – the other words all involve **showing a superior attitude toward someone or something**
f) deliberate – the other words are **all synonyms of enormous**
g) marked – the other words all **deal with the concept of doubt**

2. a) to lurk   b) crying   c) source of light (e.g., candle)   d) an inexperienced sailor
   e) a small wooded valley   f) a puncheon is a cask

Questions:

Pew, the blind beggar, returned to the inn with a number of his companions. Inside the inn, they soon found out that **Bill** was dead. The blind man and the others were upset that they did not find "Flint's fist" in the dead man's **chest**. Enraged, the men decided to scour the area, searching for **Jim** and his mother. In the midst of their search, the owners of the inn were rescued by a group of **revenue** officers. During the confusion, the blind man was killed by a **horse**. It turned out that Mr. **Dance** was the leader of the rescuers. Jim thought it best to take the paper he had saved from the chest to Dr. **Livesey**.

When Jim went to see Livesey, the magistrate was with Squire **Trelawney**. A **pigeon** pie was brought for Jim's supper. The men considered Captain **Flint** to be the blood-thirstiest buccaneer that sailed. The squire swore that he would fit out a **ship** and search for the treasure if it took a **year**. The book that Jim had taken from the trunk was the pirate's **account** book. After examining the **chart**, the men decided to go after the treasure. Jim would be the **cabin** boy. Livesey, however, was afraid that the squire would not be able to hold his **tongue**.

Language Activities:
1. We wonder if the squire's loose tongue will cause them trouble in the future.
2. Answers may vary (e.g., Eng/land).

Chapters 7 – 8: *(page 20)*
Vocabulary:
1. e   2. h   3. b   4. a   5. c   6. i   7. g   8. f   9. j   10. d

Questions:
1. The voyage to Treasure Island.
2. Hispaniola.
3. The squire had been talking too much about their plans.
4. Many interesting seamen, and the most wonderful figureheads (ships).
5. He was clean and pleasant-tempered.
6. Black Dog
7. Answers may vary (e.g., so he would give the "right" answers).
8. Black Dog got away without paying for his drink.

Language Activities:
1. Foreshadowing: "but in all my fancies nothing occurred to me so strange and tragic as our actual adventures"
2. commentaries – wives – opportunities – punches – men – stories – rigs – gentlemen
3. Answers may vary (e.g., dishonesty, critical spirit, jealous nature, gossip, insincere).

Chapters 9 – 10: *(page 23)*
Vocabulary:
1. intolerable   2. precaution   3. prosperous   4. capable   5. lanyard
6. helmsman   7. bowsprit   8. duff   9. computation   10. contrary

Questions:
1. Everyone knew more than him about the voyage; they were looking for treasure; he didn't like the crew; there was too much blabbing.
2. The squire knew he talked too much about the voyage; he was the one who chose the crew.
3. Answers may vary (e.g., he has a good point as he is responsible for the men and the voyage and if they aren't good workers he is ultimately responsible).
4. Answers may vary (e.g., perhaps the squire did mention it, or they may have found out from someone who had heard from the ones who actually buried it).
5. He was an alcoholic who wasn't very efficient at fulfilling his responsibilities. He was swept overboard.

6. Barbeque; he was a cook.
7. Answers may vary (e.g., an Amazon parrot's lifespan is about 80 years; most others live a lot less).
8. We wonder what life-threatening thing it is that Jim will hear.

Language Activities:
1. mutiny – sailor – saluted – ship – shipshape – Silver – sir – Smollett – soon - stay
2. Answers may vary. For example:
   Proper nouns: Mr. Arrow, Mr. Trelawney, Captain Smollett, Hispaniola, Dr. Livesey, Hunter, Joyce
   Adjectives: new, good, likeliest, widest, little, famous
   Pirate words: sailor, keel, captain, craft, forecastle
   Pronouns: my, them, he, his, him

Chapters 11 – 12: *(page 26)*
Vocabulary:

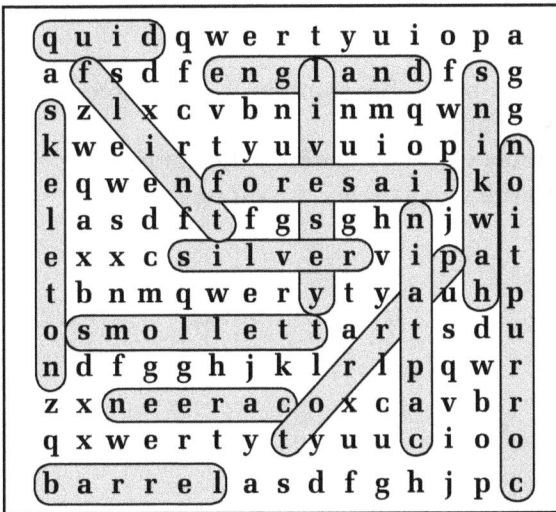

Questions:
1. The crew was going to mutiny when they reached the island and kill Jim and all his friends. Jim also learned that some members of the crew were still loyal.
2. As a safeguard, so he wouldn't raise suspicions about how he came upon so much money.
3. Since everyone knew what a bad man Flint was, Silver was saying that he was worse.
4. After the treasure was loaded aboard the ship.
5. He felt Smollett would navigate them to the island without any trouble and was unsure if they could do it as easily without him.
6. Too much hurry – and leaving witnesses.
7. He was dead.
8. He got him to call him down to the cabin where he told them the news of the pending mutiny.
9. The crew showed no signs of it beforehand.

Language Activities:
1. a) my promise   b) Dick's on our side
   c) I never saw   d) observant
2. a) The crew of the Hispaniola was overjoyed to reach Skeleton Island.
   b) Long John Silver gave Jim a ferocious glare.
   c) Why don't you go to Victoria, British Columbia, at Christmas?
   d) Aunt Eileen was born in Turkey.
   e) Chester crossed the states of Nevada and California before reaching the Pacific Ocean.

Chapters 13 – 15: *(page 29)*
Questions:
1. T   2. T   3. T   4. T   5. T   6. F   7. T   8. F   9. T   10. F

Language Activities:

1. a) It makes it seem that the coloring is a person who can be sad.
    b) The woods are called melancholy – which gives it a human emotion.
2. Answers may vary. For example:
    Person against Person: Pew and the other pirates against Jim and his mother.
    Person against Self: When Jim was in the apple barrel he was fighting against fear and the urge to escape.
    Person against Nature: Life aboard the ship battling the elements.

Chapters 16 – 17: *(page 32)*

Vocabulary:

1. besiege	2. consultation	3. leeward	4. gig	5. instincts
6. knoll	7. invaluable	8. proceeded	9. palisade	10. scuffle

Questions:

1. Dr. Livesey; to let the reader know what is going on while Jim is gone.
2. It would be good protection.
3. water.
4. He was given the chance by Captain Smollett to continue under his command, and agreed.
5. They were swept off their true course and were almost swamped.
6. Mr. Trelawney; he was asked to pick off one of the pirates who was working the cannon.
7. They were in danger of being cut off from returning to the stockade by the pirates.

Chapters 18 – 19: *(page 35)*

Vocabulary:

1. a   2. c   3. a   4. b   5. d   6. c   7. a   8. b

Questions:

1. He was shot and killed by the pirates.
2. He had been a servant.
3. Answers may vary (e.g., a show of defiance).
4. It gave them a visible target to shoot at with the ship's cannon.
5. Several months; they would not send out a rescue ship until the end of August.
6. Answers may vary (e.g., to have a written record of what had happened in the event of a court trial).
7. Silver would have flown the Jolly Roger.
8. Someone would come to meet Ben carrying a white flag in the same place that Jim had met Ben. They were to meet between noon and six bells.
9. his boat
10. He is a man with a lot of pride in himself.

Language Activities:

1. a) "If I dare," said the captain.   b) The captain made us unload the boat.
    c) ...and you're all in a lot of trouble, aren't you.   d) I'm behaving myself now.
3. molestation – molest   apologetically – apology   serviceable – service
    lying – lie   wading – wade   observation – observe
    peculiarity – peculiar   livelier – lively
4. a) Answers may vary (e.g., lots of action, make it believable).
    b) Answers may vary (e.g., Long John Silver grabbed for his cutlass and then without warning plunged it into the first mate's arm; Jim Hawkins grabbed a rope which was dangling nearby, then with his heart in his mouth, swung down from the topsail, landing right on top of Long John Silver).

Chapter 20 – 21: *(page 39)*

Vocabulary:

evident – hidden	immense – tiny	promotion – demotion	placid – stormy
absurd – logical	resumed – ceased	treacherous – loyal	

2. **a)** treacherous   **b)** promotion   **c)** absurd   **d)** immense   **e)** evident
    f) placid   **g)** resumed

Questions:
1. F   2. F   3. T   4. F   5. F   6. T   7. T   8. T   9. T   10. F

Language Activities:
1. Answers may vary. For example: nouns – muskets, tree, sand; verbs – fill, rose, running; adjectives – stunning, poor, honest.

Chapter 22 – 24: *(page 42)*

Vocabulary:
1. grievous   2. precaution   3. admirable   4. variable   5. obstinate
6. repulse   7. hawser   8. reverberations   9. supervene   10. yaw

Questions:
1. He left the fortress without a word.
2. It was a homemade, rude, lopsided framework of tough wood covered with goatskin with the hair inside.
3. He was bored and thought it would be much better to be out running free like Ben Gunn.
4. To cut the ship free so that it might drift ashore.
5. The line was too taut.
6. Answers may vary.
7. Two of the crew were drunk and fighting.
8. He was afraid he would be killed by the breakers crashing against the shore.

Language Activities:
1. **a)** It says that the boat was clever.

Chapter 25 – 27: *(page 45)*

Vocabulary:
1. c   2. a   3. d   4. b   5. c   6. a   7. b   8. d   9. a   10. c

Questions:
1. He took down the pirate flag.
2. He found two pirates – one dead, one badly injured.
3. He sent Jim to get him a drink, and then got a knife to hide in his clothing.
4. They united to bring the ship safely to shore.
5. It had gotten wet.
6. Jim shot him accidentally when Israel threw a knife at him.
7. His friends were gone and the stockade had been taken over by Silver and his men.
8. Answers may vary.

Language Activities:
1. Coxswain: petty officer; sometimes in charge of steering the ship

Chapter 28 – 30: *(page 50)*

Vocabulary:
1. freedom – the other words all have to do with **a scary feeling**
2. consumed – the other words have to do with **being relaxed**
3. talented – the other words all have to do with **being in a bad mood**
4. weak – the other words all have to do with **doing something behind someone else's back**
5. sincere – the other words all have to with **confusion**
6. enjoyment – the other words all deal with **feelings of deep dislike**
7. circumstance – the other words are all "**very active**"
8. stupendous – the other words all deal with **being unsafe**

Questions:

1. He thought they had all been killed.
2. They thought he had deserted them.
3. Answers may vary (e.g., he knew that Silver was a masterful liar and would probably see through any lies he might tell, and perhaps thought Silver would respect his honesty).
4. He probably wanted to keep his options open in case Jim's friends gained the upper hand.
5. He was being called out for a meeting.
6. When a person is on parole they are usually granted a degree of freedom after serving their sentence.
7. Answers may vary (e.g., many doctors are committed to healing everyone, regardless of personal feelings).
8. try to escape

Language Activities:

1. **a)** 5   **b)** 3   **c)** 7   **d)** 1   **e)** 2   **f)** 6   **g)** 4

Chapter 31 – 32: *(page 53)*

Vocabulary:

1. f   2. i   3. c   4. a   5. j   6. h   7. e   8. b   9. g   10. d

Questions:

1. Jim refused to try to escape when urged to by the doctor.
2. He didn't trust Silver and wondered what he was up to.
3. Find and dig up the treasure
4. a tree
5. A man's skeleton; Silver supposed it was placed in such a way that it pointed to where the treasure was buried.
6. A voice from the jungle that they thought was that of a ghost.
7. Answers may vary (e.g., Ben Gunn may have dug it up).

Language Activities:

1. without, anything, mizzenmast, itself, backward, leastways, messmates, daylight, treetops, gentleman

Chapters 33 – 34: *(page 56)*

Questions:

Before the buccaneers began digging in the pit for the treasure, Long John Silver passed Jim a **pistol**. Long John suggested that the buccaneers would only find some **pig-nuts** in the hole. George **Merry** was the leading spokesman for the pirates. The pirates were about to charge Long John and Jim when three **shots** from the thicket suddenly interrupted them. Silver was very surprised to see his old shipmate, **Ben Gunn**, with Dr. Livesey. It had turned out that Ben Gunn had carried the treasure from its burial spot to his **cave**. Just inside the mouth of the North Inlet they met the **Hispaniola**, cruising by herself. When Jim and the others finally left the island, they left the **three** mutineers behind. Even though he was still recovering from his wounds, **Captain Smollett** was still the leader on the voyage home. At a port in Spanish America, **Long John Silver** managed to escape. Only **four** men who had started the voyage to Treasure Island finally returned to England. Ben Gunn received **one thousand** pounds, which he spent or lost in **three** weeks. After the voyage, Captain Smollett **retired** from the sea, and Gray purchased a **ship**. As for Jim, for years after the voyage he dreamed of "the voice of Captain **Flint** in his dreams, "Pieces of **eight**, pieces of **eight**".